MORTGAGE MATTERS

MORTGAGE MATTERS

STRATEGIES TO SUCCESSFUL
MORTGAGE PLANNING IN A
POST MORTGAGE MELTDOWN MARKET

LOUIS SOTO

Outskirts Press, Inc.
Denver, Colorado

Dedicated to the memory of my son David

I always strived to win your admiration and approval. I am glad that we enjoyed the best 16 years anyone could have ever hoped for. I am proud to have been your father and am grateful that we could share, love and respect each other. I am hopeful that in the ages to come we will find one another again never to be torn apart by the last enemy; death.

For as in Adam all die, even so in Christ shall all be made alive.
1 Corinthians 15:22

Louis Soto is a Certified Mortgage Planning Specialist® and Vice President of Mortgage Plus Financial Group. With an extensive background in a variety of financial concentrations he has focused his attention to the development and operation of a mortgage planning practice.

In *Mortgage Matters: Strategies to Successful Mortgage Planning in a Post Mortgage Meltdown Market* Louis shares his insights on the state of the mortgage market and how to use mortgage planning strategies to avoid costly errors. The mortgage and housing landscape has changed significantly and understanding the new rules is essential to owning real estate now and in the future. Many of the ideas in this book are the result of problem solving discussions on his *"Mortgage Matters"* radio show.

Contents

AVOIDING THE PITFALLS THAT THE MASSES MADE THAT HAS LED TO RECORD FORECLOSURES—THE MADNESS BEFORE THE MELTDOWN

The American dream has become a nightmare for so many who have lost their homes or are facing foreclosure as they struggle to find a way to get caught up on mortgage arrearages. How could this happen? The excitement of shopping for a home and making the dream of homeownership a reality, the joy of finding the perfect home, decorating, furnishing and home improvement projects now overshadowed with the gloom of impending homelessness. Seemingly, overnight all has changed. Credit scores are crushed as mortgage late payments mount. Now faced with not only the disaster of losing their home, but with credit scores in the proverbial *toilet* concerns of where to relocate set in.

Who will rent to them with their credit clearly reflecting their inability to make housing payments? The emotional drain of losing a home is a defeating experience, so many feel as if they have failed themselves and their families. This is the frightful scene which has spread across our great country at an epidemic pace. With values being driven lower and more homeowners finding they owe more than their home is worth, many are opting to just walk away. The economic incentive of being a homeowner is rooted in paying your home down and building equity. With that incentive threatened the drive to press on has come to a screeching halt for many.

Many homeowners are finding that they bought at the height of an inflated real estate market and now feel like they are overpaying. In the midst of a shrinking economy the ambition of homeownership seems like a wasteful proposition. In spite of this real estate has been and continues to be a good investment, both financially and in quality of life. The problem is not with real estate or homeownership, but in how attaining it has been approached in recent years. The objective now is to understand the mistakes that were made and position ourselves not to repeat them. Learning how to buy smart will protect you from repeating or sharing in the *American scream* that so many are enduring today.

Somehow the foundation of a buying decision, which is affordability, was discounted as the real estate market prospered and everyone wanted to get in on the action. Many had a great homeownership experience as they saw the values of their homes skyrocketing unabated. Some even felt that if it went well once why not repeat the process and bought investment properties or cashed in and bought more expensive homes. With all the hype and home flipping shows becoming our new reality entertainment many decided to buy on speculation and flip or hold. There were many success stories which further fueled the excitement of the real estate market. Hard working Americans saw that while their 401k's and mutual funds weren't doing much their home seemed to continue to appreciate. If they needed more **equity**, a new appraisal would remarkably show their home value continued to grow.

With their new found equity wealth homeowners were able to finance home improvement projects, luxurious vacations, new cars and just about anything the heart desired. Values doubled yet incomes didn't. I guess that in the excitement of it all the homebuyer failed to question affordability, or ventured forth despite of it.

Banks who would typically qualify their borrowers by affordability and credit profile also thought it wasn't that important to consider affordability. Since incomes didn't keep up with the cost of homes they had to be ignored or overlooked. After all values continued to appreciate and supplement incomes as homeowners borrowed to meet their living expenses. In order to meet the demands of homebuyers who had the desire to buy, but the inability to fully prove their ability to afford; a way had to be made. Products that were once used in limited fashion for self-employed borrowers who couldn't document all of their incomes, but had assets were made available to almost anyone who expressed interest in borrowing. Stated income loans, where income is stated but not verified; no income loans, where no income is stated or verified and no ratio loans, where income is understood to be too low to qualify but ignored were made easily available.

Many loans were made without even verifying if a borrower had any income or job for that matter. Borrowers with limited and marginal credit applied for these loans and were approved. In the past only borrowers who had excellent credit and were able to put a large down payment could qualify for these kinds of loans. However, not only was poor credit ignored, little or no down payment was required. That's right, no down payment. Seemed like a scene out of a late night infomercial, no money down - 100% financing for a borrower with mediocre credit and who couldn't demonstrate their ability to repay the loan. Hundreds of thousands of dollars were transferred using this form of lending. No one seemed too concerned with affordability.

Even the rating agencies were confident that since these loans were performing well, the underlying credit risks were not a factor in how these loans - now **Mortgage Backed Securities (MBS)** would be rated. When you take out a mortgage against a home your promise to pay or mortgage note is sold on Wall Street as a MBS. Your mortgage company typically will sell your loan off to aggregators, such as Fannie Mae and Freddie Mac, or other institutional buyers who then will sell these collateralized debt obligations as MBS through Wall Street conduits. A good rating kept the floodgates of credit open and demand for this paper high. So long as Wall Street had an appetite for mortgage backed securities, banks would make the loans and borrowers would buy their homes.

Affordability was not ignored altogether. In order to keep some level of affordability banks offered and borrowers sought low rates in the form of **adjustable rate mortgages (ARM)**. Creative **negative amortization** or **interest only** loans were placed in the hands of borrowers without careful orientation or suitability requirements. Future affordability was not a concern because the borrower could simply refinance out of it, if they needed to at some point down the road. With short term rates manipulated by the **Fed** chairman at historical lows adjustable rate mortgages seemed like a good way to go.

Since affordability was an undetected problem borrowers relied on credit to make ends meet. No problem though as home values continued to grow wildly so a refinance consolidating their credit card debt or pulling out some cash was a quick fix. Borrowing against their equity to continue a lifestyle that was beyond their affordability to begin with and recycling credit card debt against mortgage debt could only last as long as home values held up and grew. However, double digit appreciation on real estate is unusual and unsustainable, so a correction would be normal, healthy and needed.

THE PERFECT STORM

As the real estate market slowed, then stalled, then pulled back the end of the road for those living from their equity became a reality. No more equity to borrow against. In the background the Fed was actively raising rates to keep inflation in check. The Fed saw it necessary to raise the Fed rate 17 times for a total of a 4.250% increase to the **Fed Funds Rate** over the course of two years. This is done to restrict or diminish credit appetite in order to slow down spending and reduce the risk of inflation. As the adjustable rate mortgages reset at the fully indexed rate which was in some cases 2-3% higher, affordability could no longer be ignored. A more detailed explanation of how rates work will be provided in chapter 7. Homeowners who used their equity through equity lines of credit saw their payments on these loans rise significantly and in many cases double. Exhausted homeowners began to falter on their mortgage payments and the reality that this class of loan would struggle as a whole sent fear through Wall Street and the appetite to buy these mortgages dried up.

As banks lost liquidity they limited or suspended these types of loans. In the past a quick **refinance** was the answer, but without the loan programs that ignore affordability many borrowers could not qualify. Compound this with lower home values and consumed and depleted equity, refinancing out of these adjustable rate mortgages or high rate loans was not an option. Additionally, **private mortgage insurance (PMI)** companies have tightened their guidelines as claims due to defaults increased, making it more difficult for borrowers to qualify. Insurance companies are experts at assessing risks and are in many cases leading the way in defining future lending criteria. Many homeowners now find themselves out of options with foreclosure looming over them.

The fundamental consideration when making any purchase is affordability. That is the case when we buy a pair of jeans and it is the case when we make the largest purchase of our lives. When evaluating when and what you're going to buy consider how much monthly mortgage payment you can comfortably handle, making concessions for the tax benefits you will gain as a homeowner. (More on that later) Consider the potential for increases in property taxes and insurance, which will increase your housing payment over time even if you have a fixed rate mortgage. Evaluate your ability to make mortgage payments in the event of an interruption in income and set aside reserves to handle life's little or not so little surprises.

DEBT TO INCOME RATIO

As the loans that ignored affordability are off the table banks are now more careful to qualify your ability to repay the loan based on **debt to income ratio (DTI)**, using verifiable income. This ratio gauges how much of your income goes toward your housing payment and how much goes to housing and consumer debt. These play a determining role in how much home you will qualify for. The qualifying DTI is impacted by your credit profile. The better the credit the more confidence the bank will have in your ability to manage credit wisely. As a result the ratio's can range anywhere from 28/36 to 50/50 or higher based on your credit and **loan to value (LTV)**. The loan to value is the ratio of debt to value against your home. DTI is represented by a front and back ratio. The front ratio measures housing payment ratio to income, whereas the back ratio shows housing and consumer debt to income ratio.

No one knows your spending habits and what you can afford better than you do. Be honest in assessing what you feel you can afford in a mortgage payment and be mindful of the consequences of ignoring this important part of the home buying process. While the experience of those who find themselves in foreclosure is a lesson to us all, it shouldn't discourage you from pursuing homeownership. When you consider the tax benefits, quality of life benefits and the return on investment in real estate we should be encouraged to pursue it all the more wisely. Even more so now that prices have corrected and make affordability more attainable. For a time many markets could no longer serve the first time homebuyer. This important homebuyer didn't have the benefit of equity from the sale of a prior home for a down payment to afford higher priced homes. I was very concerned that my children would have to move to some remote part of the country in order to pursue dreams of homeownership at the rate that real estate was appreciating. Now, with the corrections that have taken place there is improved affordability and the market will be tempered by responsible lending practices that will allow prices to appreciate moderately.

Renting may be right for some, but you'll never build equity that way or achieve the kind of leverage a homeowner has on their investment. Statistics show that homeowners typically accumulate more wealth over their lifetimes than renters. The tax code also favors homeowners enabling them to deduct housing costs that renters are not eligible for. We will address this in greater detail in chapter 7.

Here is the basic formula for calculating your debt to income ratios. In the appendix there is a worksheet you can use to help you get an accurate calculation.

$$\text{debt to income ratio} = \frac{\text{housing payment}}{\text{monthly income}} \ \& \ \frac{\text{housing payment} + \text{consumer debt}}{\text{monthly income}}$$

$$\text{loan to value} = \frac{\text{loan amount}}{\text{purchase price or appraised value}}$$
(lower of)

While the effects of this mortgage meltdown have been catastrophic for so many, it has also helped us to redefine how we approach our finances. As a result we are beginning to see credit use lessen and savings rates increase. Too often when things stabilize and the sting leaves us we return to old habits. It is important to purpose not to repeat the mistakes that got us here and commit to fiscal responsibility. Particularly, when it comes to our homes, knowing that beside the economic incentive of homeownership is a very intimate and personal experience. A home is a place where families are raised and memories made and you cannot put a price on that.

CHAPTER 2

BACK TO THE BASICS

When things fall apart or are not working the way they should, many times the solution is to go back to the basics. Here is where we find ourselves in the post mortgage meltdown market. The new way to make loans is really the old way. The days of high loan to value, mediocre credit, no income loans are gone and a return to the good old days when your credit and income determined how much you can borrow. I say "good" because everyone wins when loans are made the right way. Borrowers get loans they can repay, banks get loans that perform well, Wall Street buys these loans as mortgage backed securities which perform well for investors, real estate appreciates at ordinary rates and everyone wins.

Three basic criteria should be evaluated when making a loan: *income, credit and assets.*

When borrowing your ability to repay based on financial capability and personal responsibility are the primary concerns that a lending institution should have. As the borrower, these are vital to your decision making process as well. While the lending institution should apply due diligence in underwriting the loan and determining the risks associated with the loan the ultimate responsibility lies with you, the borrower.

You need to make sure that you don't take on more than you can handle. Ultimately, positioning yourself in a loan you cannot afford is counterproductive to the purpose you set out for when you became a homeowner. Homeownership should provide shelter and a safe haven where you can gain an improved quality of life. Obtaining a loan you cannot afford will inhibit your quality of life and ultimately leave you broke and homeless. While the good things in life often times require hard work and sacrifice, you must balance that with the quality of life benefits you gain. If the stress of a housing payment is going to cause a marriage to dissolve or make you a miserable person to be around, maybe it's time to reassess.

Once you become a homeowner a higher level of financial discipline may be required. Many times in life we find that while we have the liberty to do something we need to use restraint. Scripture says "all things are permissible, but not all are convenient." Of course the application is different, but we need to be careful knowing that not all things that are seemingly attainable are good for us in the end. Just because you can get a loan or buy that car or get this or that doesn't mean that in the long run it will be a good thing. Go slow so that you can make a wise choice. It's amazing how easy it is to convince ourselves how much better our lives will become if we buy this or that. However, in most cases we could do without. After all, once we have what we pursued feverishly we usually move on to something we don't have.

Financial capability to repay the loan is determined by income and expenses. Someone earning $3,000 per month with a $400 car payment and $150 in credit card payment can't afford a $2,000 house payment. Additional expenses such as utilities, life and auto insurance, food, transportation, entertainment and other miscellaneous items are not included in qualifying your loan affordability, but a buffer for these is allotted. Typically, a lender will be working with about 40-50% of your gross personal income as the income that you have available for a housing payment and consumer debt. Consumer debt is defined as all installment loans with greater than ten payments, auto lease payments, credit card minimum payments and student loans. Additionally, child support and alimony payments are factored into this calculation.

A quick calculation to help you get a general idea of how much housing payment you can afford is to multiply your gross monthly income by .35. The product of that calculation is what a lending institution should be looking at to start. Of course, the amount of consumer debt that you are carrying may affect the outcome. So the second consideration is calculating the consumer debt ratio, which you can do by adding consumer debt payments as defined above and dividing that by your gross monthly income. This number is ideally 10% or less. These are only general guidelines which will be subjected to the personal responsibility test by the lending institution and your own comfort test. Remember, don't take on more than you can handle.

Your housing payment will include principal and interest which is your mortgage payment and escrows from where your taxes and insurances are paid from. You will need homeowner's or hazard insurance, flood insurance if you are in a flood zone and mortgage insurance if you are using an **FHA** loan or are borrowing in excess of 80% of the lesser of your home value or purchase price. Your complete payment is known as PITI – principal, interest, taxes and insurances. An example of how this would work is:

Gross monthly income $6,500 x .35 = $2275 affordable housing payment

Total monthly consumer debt payments 600 / $6500 = 9% consumer debt ratio

(minimum credit card debt/ car & installment payments w/ greater than 10 payments, car lease)

In this example the borrower has a front ratio of 35% and a total debt ratio of 44%. Apply this formula when shopping for a home to see how your numbers work out. Lenders are not comfortable stretching these numbers too much and an overall review of credit and assets will be considered in their final underwriting decision.

The third criteria that will influence the underwriting decision are assets: the value of your home, how much you are putting down and how much you have left in reserves after closing. A higher down payment reduces the risk to the bank and reserves makes you a better risk as you will have some available cash to handle potential financial problems.

Now these numbers are all good and well, but common sense needs to be applied and someone who has demonstrated a pattern of not managing their finances well will be subjected to further scrutiny. This is where the personal responsibility test comes in. The assumption is that someone with good credit scores and overall good credit is more likely to make good financial decisions that will position them well to handle this new liability with greater responsibility. This is based on your personal past performance.

The lending institution understands that things happen, sometimes things that are outside of the control of the borrower. However, the assumption is that the good credit borrower has demonstrated an ability to judge well in their buying decisions. They have not gotten in over their heads in the past and perhaps had the financial discipline to set aside reserves for life's little or not so little surprises and weathered financial challenges well. We will discuss credit and its impact on your ability to borrow in the next chapter.

PREPARING YOUR DOCUMENTATION

Be prepared for the tougher underwriting criteria by starting a file and compiling the following items. Be careful to keep this file in a safe place as you will have an aggregate of personal information that is very personal and sensitive. I have included a check list in the appendix that can help you put your file together. You will need to get copies of W-2's for all jobs you have held over the last two years. Have copies of your signed tax returns with all schedules for that last two years. Put together a resume of all jobs you held for the last two years with contact information that will help the lending institution verify your employment and save your pay stubs. If you receive a pension, annuity or social security include copies of the award letters in your file.

If there are any gaps in employment prepare an explanation letter. Include copies of canceled rent checks to provide the bank a rental payment history and attach the names, addresses and phone numbers of your landlords for the last two years. Keep your bank statements intact as the lending institution will likely ask you for two months worth of bank statements and will require all pages of the statements. Include copies of brokerage and retirement statements. If you plan on using monies from a redemption or loan against a 401k or 403b get copies of the plan docs defining the terms under which you can borrow or redeem. Also, try not to make large deposits that you cannot explain and source.

The better you are able to document your application the easier it becomes for the bank to get a true picture of your finances. This will avoid the guess work or piece meal work that can lead to errors that could cost you in rate or program when you make a mortgage application.

The easier you make it for the bank to work your file the more attention it will get and the quicker you will have your approval and close **escrow**. When a mortgage processor or underwriter receives a file that is incomplete it will get buried under files that are more complete and easier to work. Processing and underwriting a mortgage application is a very time sensitive process. **Commitment** dates, closing dates and **rate locks** are all critical time deadlines the mortgage company is working against. As a result the files that are in condition to move will be moved. Don't attempt to reinvent or find what you may think are suitable substitutes for your documentation. It is important to provide the documentation as it is requested. Many times a borrower will provide 1 page of their bank statement with the account summary and become frustrated when it doesn't satisfy the banks requirements as the bank requires all pages. However, the bank will require complete documentation.

Obtain a copy of your credit report through the credit repositories directly as this will not count as an inquiry against you. Piling up inquiries will affect your credit score. There are a variety of credit score models that are used, to ensure that the scores you are seeing are comparable to what your mortgage lender will see go to www.myfico.com. Review your credit with a mortgage professional who can advise you how you would fair based on your credit profile and what you might be able to do to improve your credit.

Mortgage professionals often have access to credit analyzing software that can give you a good idea of what steps you can take to increase your scores efficiently and expediently. It's a different world out there now. Due to more rigorous underwriting criteria good credit has never been more important when qualifying for financing and getting the best deal. Even those with excellent credit are finding that it has become difficult to match a program to their profile. Ensuring that you have the best possible credit will better position you to find a program that fits your needs.

Be careful of credit repair companies, credit counseling, or debt settlement companies. Often times these programs cause credit to go delinquent and scores suffer. If you feel that there is something to be gained by these services have a third party review their proposals. Consult with someone versed in credit practices, like a qualified mortgage planner or other financial professional or attorney.

It's never too early to start preparing. Understand that this is probably the largest investment of your life and although common should not be taken lightly. If you had inherited hundreds of thousands of dollars you would be very careful as to how you would invest these dollars and ensure good counsel. The same care should be taken when borrowing hundreds of thousands of dollars. You are about to add an asset to your balance sheet worth hundreds of thousands of dollars and a liability of comparable size. Getting an early start on preparing for your home purchase or refinance will help you make better decisions and get the best possible financing.

CHAPTER 3

CREDIT CRUNCH CAUSES CREDIT CRITIRIA TO BE CRITICALLY CHALLENGED

Financial markets are driven by two basic human emotions: fear and greed. Greed was the dynamic force that drove Wall Streets appetite for higher yielding mortgage backed securities. The risk factor seemed tolerable as the rating agencies found little fault with them. Greed drove banks to find new ways to make more of this very saleable paper. Like a pendulum swinging out of control the emotion shifted quickly to fear once concerns of the solvency of the borrowers began to surface.

Wall Street no longer had the same demand for this paper and the lenders find their shelves stocked with paper they cannot move. Mortgage banks rely on liquidity for their survival. If they cannot get closed loans off their books they cannot make new loans. For over 50,000 lending institutions this meant a substantial pull back of their lending practices or closing their doors. Banks received Wall Street downgrades and margin calls were made as a lot of the loans made by banks were made with other people's money and the only way to pay for these liabilities is to off-load the loans they made.

However, with no takers the banks couldn't meet their obligations and were forced out of business. Without knowing where the bottom is, revisions to lending guidelines are released regularly as lenders and Wall Street try to find the safe zone short of crawling into a fetal position. In all fairness, while there have been some knee jerk reactions to the devastation the mortgage markets were hit with, the overall response has been one of sudden sobriety and a return to smart lending practices.

You would think that a **collateralized debt obligation (CDO)** would not have such an impact on the markets. After all if the debt doesn't perform the underlying asset guaranteeing the debt can be seized and sold. While there may be some losses the asset should cover a large part of the underlying debt. However, our monetary system is based on fiat currency. When our banking system originated banks offered notes as a substitute for gold. Americans would deposit their gold with a banker who would charge a fee for storage and issue a note. This provided greater convenience and safety. Bankers soon realized that while people were depositing their gold and later cash, few ever returned to cash in their notes and so issuing notes on margin began. This is where the banker would issue more notes than the gold collateralized. If everyone cashed in their notes at the same time this would be a problem but was unlikely. This same idea has been applied to the notes that are guaranteed by mortgages across America, as derivatives on this paper are created and sold the collateral is marginalized.

You may have a home mortgage note with derivatives many times its worth and when you don't have too many defaults the market can bear this, however an increase in defaults has an exponential impact on the market. Can you imagine how the banks would react if depositors made a rush to withdraw their deposits. This would be a problem and so it is with collateralized debt obligations such as mortgage notes when the tolerable number of defaults is surpassed.

HOW GOOD IS YOUR CREDIT

Creditworthiness is a core component to smart underwriting and as fear pervades the mortgage markets it is very important to get your credit in tip top shape. Whereas, marginal credit was sufficient a short time ago having excellent credit is critical to ensuring that you are finance-able and that you get a good rate at a fair price.

Today **FNMA** and **Freddie Mac**, which are the largest buyers of mortgages have and continue to modify lending criteria and have added additional risk based pricing. What this means is that even if you have good credit you may still need to pay a premium to get the loan. This will drive your rate up in order to account for the premium pricing or cost you additional points to keep the rate at its base price.

RISK BASED PRICING

For example, someone with a middle credit score under 700 may need to pay a point if they were putting 25% down. A point is equal to 1% of your loan amount. This will mean that in order to get the market rate you would need to pay that point or take a rate an eighth to a quarter higher to absorb that cost. The cost at this time increases to as much as 2.75 points the lower your credit goes. These were costs good credit borrowers didn't have to contend with prior to the mortgage melt-down.

Beside credit scores your credit's depth is subject to greater scrutiny. The number of trade lines, how long you've had them and how well you have managed them is being reviewed more carefully. Obtaining a copy of your credit reports from all three bureaus is simple and inexpensive and can help you be better prepared for your mortgage application. You can get these reports on demand at Experian.com, Transunion.com and Equifax.com.

Review your credit and dispute online any discrepancies or inaccurate information. This is all done with a click of your mouse. The credit bureaus will initiate an investigation that will be resolved within 30 days. There is no reason why your mortgage should be negatively impacted by inaccurate information on your credit.

Be selective when allowing others to run your credit as too many inquiries will be interpreted as an act of financial despair on you part driving your scores down. Do not close any accounts, but look to pay down your credit balances. The older the account the more it can affect your credit score positively. The idea is that the longer you have had an account open the more time you have had to screw things up. Managing a credit account successfully over a longer period of time will boost your credit scores.

IMPROVING YOUR CREDIT SCORES

Paying down your credit cards to get your balance to available credit ratio as low as possible will help your scores dramatically and quickly. Getting your balances at 30% or lower than your credit lines will help boost your scores. You can improve your score 100 points or more in many cases by keeping this balance to available credit ratio low.

Some people will favor their lower interest rate cards, which is understandable. However, if this causes your balance to available credit ratio to be high on a card it could impact you negatively. It would be better to spread your debt over all cards for credit score purposes to keep the ratios low.

If you have cosigned on a loan for someone, obtain canceled

checks from them evidencing that they are making payments so that your debt to income ratio is not affected by someone else's debt. While this item will continue to appear on your credit report, presenting this evidence to your mortgage lender will enable the liability not to be counted against you. If there is any negative credit on your credit report that you have resolved provide evidence of this to the credit bureaus reflecting this information.

Most mortgage companies have the ability to have your credit report rescored if you provide them with documentation to have your credit corrected. This can be pricey as the credit agency charges per account and per bureau. Getting your own report and working on clearing any issues early will save you money and aggravation later.

IMPROVING YOUR DEBT RATIO

Consider how your payments will impact your debt to income ratio and look to pay off those liabilities with the highest payment to debt ratio first. Divide your minimum payment by the balance to get the payment rate and pay down the items with the highest payment rate first.

For example, assume you have a credit card with a $3,000 balance that has a minimum payment of $85.00 and an installment loan of $1,500 with a monthly payment of $70. Your monthly payment rate on the credit card is .028 where as the payment rate on the installment loan is .046. The loan has a lower payment but a higher payment rate which impacts your debt to income ratio more significantly.

A good way to attack this debt is to pay the installment loan down to $700 so that you would have less than 10 payments left eliminating the debt from counting as a liability against your debt to income ratio altogether. However, if your concern is not debt to income ratio but credit score you may be better off paying down the credit card to reduce the balance to available credit ratio.

Lenders base their credit score requirements off of the middle of your three scores. If you are financing with a co-borrower the lower of your two middle scores is used. So when considering actions to boost your scores target the credit reported on the bureau that has issued you the middle score. There are some benchmarks that you want the middle score to exceed to get better pricing and terms. The credit score benchmarks are 740, 720, 700, 680, 660, 640 and 620. Being a point below the next bracket is enough to cost you thousands of dollars.

Do not make any purchases on credit while you are preparing to make a mortgage application. This is a good practice at any time. The idea of buying depreciating assets and paying many times its original value due to high interest rates is a formula for poverty. This avoids the inquiries to your credit and the strain to your debt to income ratio caused by higher liabilities.

As odd as it may sound, defer paying off collection and charged off accounts if you are preparing to make a mortgage application. Paying them could cause your credit scores to drop as the date of last activity becomes more current. A better idea may be to make application first prompting the lender to pull credit and then pay off these accounts using certified funds so that you can document the accounts paid to your lender. This will establish your scores prior to paying off your collection and charged off accounts which could temporarily lower your scores. Also, note that these accounts may be very negotiable and you may be able to pay these off at a fraction of the debt.

Prepare a credit explanation letter for all negative credit and inquiries and attach pertinent documentation to it. Even if you have paid off negative credit it carries forward. Your payment history stays with you for 7 years and 10 years on judgments, foreclosures and bankruptcy. The time starts ticking after you pay-off judgments, collection and charged off accounts.

This means that negative credit could reflect on your credit for a very long time. Some people assume that since they have paid off a collection, charge-off or judgment that it is now good credit. However, while you paid – you paid late and that is not a good thing. Locate warrant of satisfactions on any paid judgments and if you've had a bankruptcy include the BK paperwork, all filed schedules, list of creditors and discharge.

If you do not have many open and active trade lines make charges against any open accounts that don't show current activity to re-activate reporting. Obtain alternative trade line payment history letters. These are payment history letters from creditors that don't typically report to the credit bureaus such as phone companies, utility companies, Cable Company, etc. This can help beef up your credit profile. These items will not show on your permanent credit file but the credit agency your mortgage company is using will add it to their report. The report the underwriter reviews to make an underwriting decision will be a supplemented version that reflects your payment history for these alternative trade lines and may be considered as a compensating factor.

While the past is not a guarantee of future performance, it is the only way a lending institution can predict how you will man-age the credit they are issuing. If your credit suffers any kind of damage it will take years to season it. Be careful not to take this lightly as credit is very fragile, even the small oversight of paying a $15 credit card bill 30 days late can significantly impact your credit scores.

This could cost you a lot of money as risk based pricing is as-sessed to your mortgage interest rate. Doing some preliminary groundwork on your credit is essential to ensuring that you get the best terms when applying for a mortgage. This holds true even if you have very good credit as the new benchmarks for pricing conforming loans is making loans more expensive for borrowers across the board.

CHAPTER 4

INCOME DOCUMENTATION AND ALTERNATIVE STRATEGIES

The most basic form of loan is a full-documentation loan. A borrower applying for this kind of loan is expected to be able to document their current and past two years income. Documentation of income comes in the form of pay stubs, W-2's, tax returns, pension award letters and court validation for child support and alimony. An additional layer of verification will come in the form of validation of your documentation with the IRS. It is common to sign IRS form 4506 which authorizes the lender to verify your income documentation with the IRS. The lender may also obtain written verification of your income from your employer.

DESK TOP UNDERWRITING

The amount of required documentation hinges on what the computer asks for. Loan applications are now underwritten by a computer first; using FNMA or Freddie Mac automated underwriting known as **Desktop Underwriter (DU)** and **Loan Prospector (LP)**, respectively.

The findings determine what documentation will be necessary to underwrite your loan. A human underwriter will then validate that the documentation you submitted supports the data that you have provided on your application. In some cases a manual underwrite is allowed, but this is rare now. An underwriter is free to request additional documentation if it is necessary to make the underwriter comfortable that the borrower can and will repay this loan. The better the credit is, the lighter the documentation burden.

For self-employed borrowers the personal income and not the business income is what is used to evaluate your income qualifications. This is an important differentiation as many times people are confident that they can qualify for a mortgage and base that on their total revenue, but it is that income minus business expenses that transfers over as personal income on your 1040 form. If you make $100,000, but write off $50,000 in business expenses the bank feels that you are not able to rely on the full $100,000 of income as you need to invest $50,000 in order to make the 100k. They will take your net business income as the amount you have available to you to pay for personal expenses such as your mortgage. If you are not self-employed but are paid on a 1099 basis this rule applies as well. This is when your employer is not withholding taxes. While you may be performing the duties of an employee you are essentially considered self-employed. Your income would be averaged over the last two years whereas a salaried W-2 employee is typically qualified based on current income. Rental income can also be used to qualify if you are buying a multifamily. Between 75 – 85% of the market rent can be used as income to help qualify for your loan.

The importance of documenting your income and validating the documentations veracity is essential to determining what you qualify for. Your debt to income ratio can be fine tuned as the underwriter reviews your income. Salaries are calculated differently than bonus, commission, overtime, and business income. These are usually averaged over two years. As a result your actual debt to income ratio is usually not fully understood until all income documentation is received, tabulated and recalculated. Pensions, annuities, child support and alimony will only be counted if you will continue to receive this income for at least the next three years. Child support and alimony need to have a one year payment history and dividend income must be averaged over the prior two years. As some of your income may not be eligible to be counted your debt to income ratio may be challenged to the point of an adverse pricing effect or outright disqualification.

There is still some limited availability of limited or no doc loans, however the criteria for these loans usually require larger down payments or lower loan to value ratios, higher credit scores, and appraisals undergo additional scrutiny. Preference is given to self-employed borrowers as it is assumed that wage earners can usually document their income.

Proving that you are self employed will be required if you are claiming so. A letter from your CPA, business license, phone directory listing and other forms of proof may be required. It is not uncommon for an underwriter to Google you or your businesses as it is assumed that a business relies on marketing in order to generate business. Additionally, a stated income loan needs to pass a reasonability test. The income being stated should be a representation of your true income. The underwriter will look at income averages for your occupation in order to determine the sensibility of the income you are stating. To see what they may see you can check www.salary.com to get an idea of how your stated income compares to the median income for your occupation in your area.

There are some borrowers who cannot qualify for limited documentation loans, although they might have bought their home with this kind of loan. The use of a co-borrower might be the only option for a borrower who cannot prove enough personal income to qualify on their own. The co-borrowers income can help you qualify for a full-documentation loan and in some cases, even the use of a non-occupying co-borrower might be sufficient to help you qualify.

ALTERNATIVE STRATEGIES

Again, let me stress the importance of using common sense. Just because you can get the loan doesn't mean that you can pay it. Co-borrowers should only be used when the co-borrowers understand that they are making a commitment to pay for that loan in the event of default. The co-borrower should have the willingness and ability to help you pay for the mortgage, if necessary. The use of a co-borrower to qualify for a loan should only be employed if you know that you have the income to pay but cannot document it.

In some cases where the borrower does not receive pay stubs. A lender may accept a letter from the employer explaining how the borrower is paid as sufficient documentation. If credit is superior and loan to value is low the underwriting requirement may be employment verification only which minimizes your documentation requirements even further. Remember that providing accurate income information is essential to determining how much mortgage payment you can reasonably pay.

2/1 BUY DOWN

If you find that you are having difficulty qualifying for the loan that you are applying for consider a 2/1 buy down. This is an approach that will have you prepay interest in order to get a lower rate in years one and two. This is a fixed graduated payment. You will qualify based on the rate in the first year. An example of this might be a rate of 5% in the first year, 6% in the second year and 7% for the balance of the loan. You can negotiate the cost of the prepaid interest to be paid by the lender or seller of the home.

Typically when you pay **discount points** it will reduce your rate by a .250% or so for the life of the fixed term for every point that you pay. With the buy down the impact is more dramatic in the first two years as you are reducing your interest rate by a full 2% in the first year and 1% in year two. The rate on these loans will be higher in years 3-30 but not subject to fluctuation as it is a fixed rate mortgage. This is a more sound and predictable method as compared to many who opted for adjustable rate mortgages and exposed themselves to the unpredictability of a volatile and rising interest rate environment. With this program you can get into the home and ease into the higher payments. Usually, the first few years of homeownership are burdened with furnishing expenses. Many end up financing their furnishings with high interest rate, non-tax favored loans or revolving credit and bear the cost of these purchases for many years. Using this type of program you can maximize cash flow to afford the set up of your new home without relying on credit and perhaps set up an emergency mortgage fund. It's wise to always maintain a reserve account with several months' mortgage payments to protect against foreclosure.

An interesting note about negotiating points to be paid by the seller is that you still get the tax deduction even though you didn't directly pay for the points. It also reduces the potential tax implications of the sale of the home to the seller. This is a true win-win situation. This strategy can help you ease into homeownership and qualify for a bit more loan than you can qualify for now. Because the increases are predictable you can make provision for them before it becomes a problem.

This kind of loan works well for those that anticipate an increase in income in the near future, perhaps rental income that will become available after you own the home or a relative who will be moving in and helping with payments. Maybe you will be getting married soon and will have someone partnering in the payment or are getting a promotion or perhaps have a spouse returning to work.

While you are having the benefits of a lower payment it would be wise to set aside that savings into a reserve account. To calculate your cost vs. savings simply calculate your mortgage at the full rate then 2 % lower and subtract the difference. Repeat for year two by calculating your mortgage at 1% below the full rate and subtract from the full payment. You can now see what your payment will look like in year one, two and the balance of the term. Add the difference of the annualized payments in year one and two to get cost of the buydown. You can use mortgage calculators that are found all over the web to work up your payments.

For example:

Full payment at 6.5% on 200k loan = $1264 (a)

Year one at 4.5% =   1013 (b)

Year two at 5.5% =   1135 (c)

Apply the following formula
$(a - b) + (a - c)$ to get your buy down cost.

Another option is to carefully consider FHA's adjustable rate programs as they have very low **margins** and your rate can only increase by 1% per year. With FHA's streamline program you can refinance out of the adjustable if you need to with limited qualification criteria and costs. Beware that there are criteria is continually changing and may become more stringent. This is further explained in chapter seven. By using this less volatile and more safeguarded adjustable rate mortgage you can finance your home more affordably or qualify for more home. Again, be mindful that if you are qualifying for more home that you need to ensure that you have other resources available in the event your mortgage adjusts to a higher payment and other financing options are not immediately available to you.

Location, location, location is to real estate as documentation, documentation, documentation is to a mortgage application. Keep good records and be prepared to provide your mortgage lender with all of the documentation they may need. This will ensure that you know quickly what you will qualify for and save you money in appraisal and inspection fees. You wouldn't want to spend money on inspections and set your heart on your dream home only to find out later that you don't qualify. Your sellers may also be incurring costs on their potential purchase which will be lost to them if you don't qualify.

CHAPTER 5

NEW PROGRAMS TO HELP US COPE?

For many years those borrowers who had marginal credit and little down payment monies, but could demonstrate enough income to handle their mortgage payment would be able to finance their homes using FHA insured loans. The Federal Housing Administration (FHA) is a government agency that insures loans for borrowers who have little toward a down payment; many have had some credit issues and may have a high debt to income ratio. The debt to income ratio could be a bit higher for an FHA loan than it may be on a **conventional loan**.

Essentially, it is a higher risk loan backed by a government agency that affords a segment of the home buying community with a chance at home ownership, managed by a premium the borrower pays on their loan, known as mortgage insurance. Banks are more likely to lend knowing that the government will guarantee the loan. FHA has played a very important part in making homeownership affordable and possible for many lower income families and has helped to rebuild lower income communities.

However, due to increasing home values that outpaced income growth this segment of the home buying community was easier served with no income verification loans at 100% financing.

Additionally, FHA loan limit restrictions made this program impractical in high priced areas.

Many of these loans were structured as 80/20 loans – an 80% 1st mortgage and a second mortgage covering the balance of the home purchase with no insurance to offset the risk of this higher risk loan. The rates on these loans were usually 7-8% on an adjustable 1st mortgage and 10-14% on the second mortgage. While the borrower didn't have to pay mortgage insurance these loans carried a higher cost and the unpredictability of an adjustable rate. Had these loans fit the FHA model the rate would have been in the 6-7% range on a fixed rate mortgage. The borrower would have been in a safer mortgage as well as the banks issuing them. Additionally, mortgage backed securities that are backed by FHA loans are guaranteed by **Ginnie Mae**. These mortgage backed securities carry the security of the full faith and credit guarantee of the US government.

Think about how things might have played out if all of those **subprime** and **Alt-A** loans that perished or faltered sending shrills through Wall Street and drying up liquidity to the banks had been guaranteed. The right kind of loans would have been made. There would have been significantly fewer defaults as homeowners would have acquired more affordable mortgages with fixed rates. Investors would feel safer and continue to buy these mortgage backed securities, banks would be able to sell off their mortgages and stay in business.

Homeownership would have continued to be positively fostered as more people would continue to have enjoyed a good homeownership experience. Last but not least, home prices would have been supported by a healthy mortgage financing industry.

As the FHA program appeared to be outdated more and more obtained their loans with creative programs that seemed to keep up with current market needs. Of course, with higher rates and many of these being adjustable rates on no equity home purchases in a flat and declining real estate market the $#!+? hit the fan and it made a big mess. The US and global markets have been impacted as these mortgages, that collateralized mortgage back securities are the hot potato that no one wants. Those getting stuck with them got burned and many had to close shop. Banks that are in the business of lending money must manage the risks associated with the loan they are making. In past years private mortgage insurance companies and the FHA helped to offset potential losses in a defaulted loan. However on these 80/20 loans the second lien holder; the lender servicing the second mortgage found they no longer had much lien power as there wasn't any asset left to cover the lien in a deteriorating real estate market. While no one wants to lose their home there is little incentive to keep someone bound to a home when they owe more on it than it's worth.

Most now realize that this segment of the home buying community is served best with the FHA program. These loans are in favor with the lending industry again. FHA has undergone revision under the FHA Modernization Act and is meeting the needs of a larger segment of homeowners. More borrowers will be able to finance their homes with a fixed rate, using a small down payment on purchases with the proper risk coverage insuring these loans. Higher loan limits will also allow more people to use the advantages of this program to finance their homes.

FHA SECURE

In the meantime, the government authorized the FHA Secure program enabling those who were hit with payment shock due to an adjustable rate mortgage to refinance into a low fixed rate mortgage. The catch is that the borrower needs to demonstrate that any late mortgage payments in excess of two thirty day late payments are the result of an adjustment in the mortgage payment. Additionally, proposals to insure existing non-FHA loans facing foreclosure may be worked out with many lenders. Modifying these loans could keep many out of foreclosure. However, this program was ineffective and subsequently abandoned.

STIMULUS PACKAGE

The government has opened up FHA to insure and FNMA and Freddie Mac to buy loans in excess of the conforming and FHA County limits up to loan amounts of $729,250. This has created a new class of loan known as FHA and Agency **Jumbo loans** which have widened the availability of affordable loan programs to many. As jumbo loans became very expensive this new class of jumbo loan is helping many get into low fixed rate mortgages. This can help those with multiple loans exceeding conforming limits consolidate into a lower cost single mortgage. Although set forth as a temporary program, a version of this more expanded lending should become permanent to allow for continued support of larger loans, particularly in high priced areas.

Additionally, the ability to refinance loans that are upside down or have high loan to value ratios has become available, enabling those who can qualify to refinance were it not for a value issue. This is helping many who were stuck with higher than market interest rates get lower rates and improving their finances.

FHA has seen an emergence in demand. It's interesting that when the easy to get 80/20 loan market dried up the consumer found their way back to the loan program that they should have been in to begin with.

DOWN PAYMENT ASSISTANCE

Several years ago, in response to a segment of FHA homebuyers who didn't have down payment monies, down payment assistance programs became available. Programs such as Nehemiah, where a non-profit agency agrees to grant the borrower the down payment monies in exchange for a donation received by the seller from the proceeds of the sale gained popularity. FHA allows the borrower to use gift monies to meet the required statutory investment of 3.5%. FHA's only limitation to this gift is that it cannot come from the seller. Since the DPA program is granting the monies prior to receiving the donation it is deemed different money and borrowers can in effect get into a home with no down payment.

These programs were prohibited in late 2007, only to win a judicial appeal and once again outlawed as an acceptable way to help those with no down payment get into low fixed rate FHA insured loans. These programs may return in the future, but for now you will need to deposit 3.5% down in order to qualify for FHA financing. This can come from a gift but not from the seller of the home. Perhaps requiring reserves might be a better way to manage the risks associated with borrowers with no down payment. After all if a borrower gets into trouble they would weather it better if they had savings to draw from rather than trapped equity. The borrower who exhausted all of their resources to muster up the necessary down payment may be a greater risk than one who put less down but has a reserve. There was talk of FHA insuring 100% financed loans in the future, but for now it seems that it is off the table.

A tax rebate is helping some folks get into homes. In most cases the borrower will still need to come up with their down payment, but can receive up to $8,000 back in the form of a tax rebate. This is a temporary program that was extended and enhanced in 2009 and again in 2010, but only for part of the year.

There was a time that FHA required home ownership counseling; perhaps a return to this will help potential homeowners understand homeownership better. Equipping people with debt management and budgeting skills is obviously needed and can help many avoid the pitfalls that lead to financial trouble.

An increasing number of borrowers continue to face challenges finding mortgage financing. Risk based interest rates and the lack of flexibility of banks and mortgage insurance companies with regard to income documentation has left a large segment of homeowners with few or no financing options. In time this demand will need to be filled. Of course, until the economy and housing market in particular stabilizes, consumer confidence improves, and wounds heal we are working with a very narrow selection of mortgage product.

700,000,000,000 AND GROWING?

Those are a lot of zeros. That is how much the government has committed to bail Wall Street and banks out of this mess. However, while this may strengthen faltering banks and financial companies I don't know that it will do much to correct the problem that supposedly caused all of the trouble. If the problem lies in borrowers defaulting on their mortgages as a result of a declining market and increasing interest rates, perhaps addressing throwing money in that direction would have been a better solution. If the money is going to be spent may as well spend it wisely. Since the problem was that homeowners stopped making their mortgage payments addressing that problem should result in a solution. Consider that there are many Americans who find themselves upside down on a mortgage with bad terms to boot.

Where is the incentive to keep up with their mortgage payments in a time of economic duress? Perhaps a better way to get these monies to the banks would have been to filter it through the homeowner, by helping them to negotiate a debt that was more in line with current values and getting second mortgages paid at a discount.

Second mortgages are often negotiated down to next to nothing in foreclosure proceedings. Banks would jump all over the opportunity to get something now rather than nothing later and get these off their books. Homeowners would own a home where the value was more in line with the liability and free up the dollars they were using to pay on second mortgages which would serve to solidify their cash flow and overall finances. With more disposable income available and home prices in line with their corresponding liability economic growth and consumer confidence are promoted. This would trickle up, down and through the economy strengthening families and corporations alike.

CHAPTER 6

QUALIFYING FOR A GOOD RATE—EVEN WITH BAD CREDIT

It is neither uncommon nor unreasonable that a borrower with bad credit earn a higher interest rate due to the amount of work that goes into originating and processing that loan and the higher risk in servicing that loan. Even though FHA might insure this type of loan offsetting the risks, the mortgage company may be concerned that a default would increase costs related to collection.

Also, a lender with too many defaulted FHA loans may find that they lose the authority to make these types of loans. As a result some lenders have more restrictive, self imposed FHA financing guidelines than FHA requires.

While a borrower may find that a higher rate may be the consequence of negative credit. With an FHA mortgage a higher rate translates to a rate a half to one percent higher than market rates. Certainly, still better than sub-prime rates which are nowhere to be found at this time. Adjustable rate mortgages can be risky, but for the right borrower FHA has adjustment restrictions and easy to refinance provisions that make it a tolerable risk if you find the need to take an adjustable due to higher fixed rate costs.

When an FHA underwriter looks at your application they are looking for your ability to make your mortgage payments based on the same criteria we have established in earlier chapters. Can you and will you make your payments? To determine this they will evaluate your income vs. liabilities and your credit. FHA has more lenient underwriting criteria and debt to income ratios can be higher as a result.

Credit problems are understood within reason. It is important that you be able to isolate the problem that led to the credit problems and convince the underwriter that you have everything under control at this time. FHA can be underwritten using DU and LP; however some manual underwriting is still applied to these loans. Additionally, loans that are referred to a human underwriter can be fully manually underwritten, whereas their conventional counterpart will not manually underwrite.

FHA 203K REHAB

FHA also allows you to finance home improvement and renovation in excess of the current value of your home but within the future value after repairs. This is known as a 203k loan and can help those with already tight budgets get into a home that will have little future maintenance costs. Many find that after buying a home they are faced with expensive, but necessary repairs that put a strain on their ability to make timely mortgage payments.

They may not be able to make the repairs or go into non tax favored high cost loans to get the work done. A better option is to consider this program on the onset so that you avoid sudden repair costs in the near future. Also this expands the possibilities when shopping for a home as the home that you would pass on now becomes the diamond in the rough. You can make buying an older home similar to buying a custom new construction as you can make the renovations to your specifications. Consider this when you find that home that is perfect, but needs a new roof or siding or simply has that lime green tile that you can't live with.

This program also helps those that are financing a mixed-use property. A mixed-use property is one where there are residential units attached to a commercial unit. This type of property usually requires a large down payment, has higher costs to acquire and higher interest rates as it is viewed as a commercial property. By using the 203k program you can finance a mixed-use property with little down and with monies for repairs at a good rate that will qualify for a further improved interest rate once the work is completed. Interest rates are usually a bit higher for this program.

FHA STREAMLINE

One of the most borrower friendly programs in the market is a streamline FHA refinance. This is for FHA to FHA loans only. The advantage is that the borrower doesn't have to prove income or assets and credit review is usually limited to mortgage payment history. Cost for this loan is minimal and many times absorbed by the lender.

This is a very valuable program as you can get into lower rates as they become available without the costs that may otherwise preclude you from refinancing. You can do this as often as you would like to take advantage of lower rates. There are some impending changes that may make it a bit more challenging to qualify, but for now it is a great way to get into lower interest rates with little or no closing costs and minimal qualification criteria.

Additionally, if you had to take a higher rate due to credit issues within a few months you may qualify to streamline into the lower market rates without having the documentation that caused your higher rate follow you into the new loan. If you have a higher rate due to a 203k rehab loan you can streamline into a regular FHA loan, also known as a 203b loan upon completion of your rehab project. This will also enable to reduce your rate subject to market conditions.

Using this two step approach can put you into a very low fixed rate with an affordable mortgage payment. Remember, you qualify and may only need to pay closing costs once and then can streamline as often as you'd like to avail yourself of declining rates.

Another way to get a lower rate is to use a 15 year FHA loan with a 90% or lower loan to value. Not only are the rates usually a half percent or so lower than 30 year fixed rates, you don't have monthly mortgage insurance costs which lowers your effective rate on your mortgage. Many who buy with little down will be able to qualify for this program as their home appreciates. The absence of the mortgage insurance cost and lower interest rate could be the combination that helps you become mortgage free in a shorter time.

Of course, don't take on more than you can handle. You wouldn't want the hopes of paying off your mortgage early be the cause of financial hardship and subsequent default. I usually recommend a side investment account over a 15 year amortization where you are accumulating greater equity outside of the mortgage lien. This is a strategy we will discuss later to help you protect your equity. However, having the lower rate and no mortgage insurance may be the right move for you. Consulting your mortgage professional in conjunction with your financial planner can help you make the right decision for you.

CHAPTER 7

UNDERSTANDING HOW THE FED AFFECTS MORTGAGE RATES

Let's start out by looking at how rates work. A fixed mortgage is a mortgage that has an interest rate that is fixed for the life of the mortgage. Usually, this rate is a bit higher because you are asking the bank to guarantee the rate which may cause interest rate risk to the bank if interest rates rise. This is because as rates rise the appeal for your mortgage diminishes as there are higher yielding mortgages in the market. An adjustable rate mortgage (ARM) is usually fixed for a certain period than recasts at a different rate based on interest rates at the time of adjustment thus limiting interest rate risk to the lender.

UNDERSTANDING ADJUSTABLE RATES

Adjustable rate mortgages carry three separate rates that you need to pay careful attention to. Most people are familiar with their starting interest rate, but do not know what the other two underlying rates are. The other two play a more important role as they will determine future interest rates on your mortgage for a greater duration than the start rate. Knowing what these rates are can help you plan better for potential increases to your mortgage interest rate.

One of the internal rates is known as the margin which is fixed for the life of the loan and set at the time of the loan origination. This margin can sometimes be negotiated to protect against future increases to your mortgage payment. The second internal rate is tied to an index, such as the **Treasury, COFI, COSI, MTA, LIBOR** or **Prime;** all of which are variable. These are published rates which you can find in any financial publication. A simple way to keep your eye on the index that will impact your future rate is at www.armindexes.com. If you aren't sure what index your ARM is tied to review a copy of your mortgage note and the margin and index will be there. At the time of adjustment the bank simply adds the index to your margin to get the new rate. This is why it is important to negotiate the lowest margin whenever possible. Considering the type of index your mortgage is based on is important as some indexes are more volatile than others. Libor, Prime and Treasury are quicker movers compared to COFI, COSI and MTA.

In a market where the Fed is lowering rates you may want an index which is more responsive so that you get the benefit of the lower rates more quickly. Conversely, in a market where the Fed is or is likely to be raising rates you would want to be tied to an index that is less responsive to delay the rise of your interest rate. Libor and Prime rates are the most reactive indexes, whereas a COFI, COSI, and MTA are slower to respond to changes the Fed makes in the monetary policy. Most adjustable mortgages have caps on the amount that your rate can be increased to minimize payment shock risk.

An example might be someone who is borrowing using a 5/1 LIBOR adjustable rate mortgage at 5.5% with a 2.750 margin. The loan is fixed at 5.5% for the first five years as the name implies. At the end of this period the margin of 2.750 is added to the current index rate to get the new rate applied to your balance at that time. Assuming the LIBOR is at 5.250 at the time of adjustment your rate would be 8% were it not for the 2% cap which limits the hike to a rate of 7.5% until the next adjustment.

The Federal Open Market Committee led currently by Ben Bernanke whose predecessor was Alan Greenspan can help to influence the direction of interest rates. This is done primarily to help keep inflation under control. During a time of inflation the likely culprit is an economy of excess disposable income and low cost credit which spurs consumers to buy everything in sight, hence producing an increase in prices due to demand otherwise known as inflation. Inflation depletes the value of the dollar affecting your buying power. Everyone remembers how our grandparents told tales of nickel loaves of bread. Some interesting illustrations of inflation are looking back 50 years in history and finding that a stamp cost 3 cents, a loaf of bread 19 cents and a gallon of gasoline 20 cents. As prices go up our ability to buy products and services are diminished.

When economic indicators raise inflationary concerns the Fed will impose a restrictive monetary policy to slow down spending and keep inflation under control. Economic indicators such as the **Consumer Price Index (CPI)**, unemployment and jobless claims are watched carefully to gauge the direction of consumer confidence. When the economy is sluggish the Fed would look to promote an accommodative monetary policy by lowering rates and making credit more affordable, which encourages spending which fuels the economy and creates jobs.

The rate the government regulates is the Fed Funds Rate, which is not a mortgage rate. So how does the Fed's activity make its way into the mortgage markets? Many people feel that when the Fed lowers or raises rates it will automatically have an effect on their mortgage in like manner.

However, while the Fed's activity affects other short term rates such as the Prime and Libor it relies on market reaction for the true outcome of how mortgage rates respond to its actions. When the Fed lowers rates it will almost always have a positive effect on these short term rates which are the very indexes adjustable mortgages are tied to. This is good as it will lower your adjustable mortgage rate and make adjustable rates more affordable. Conversely, the Fed raising rates would more than likely have an adverse effect.

FIXED RATE MORTGAGES

When you borrow money against a mortgage you are usually borrowing for the long term, in most cases 30 years. Although the life of most mortgages is significantly shorter you could hold the bank to the original terms for 30 years. This 30 year mortgage note is sold as a mortgage backed security that guarantees a cash flow to an investor. Investors are always concerned about the rate of return they will get and how this rate of return could be affected by inflation. If inflation becomes a problem it will erode the cash flow from their investment which affects the cash flows buying power. Also, it will affect the future value of the principal dollars when they are returned to the investor at a later date.

When Wall Street is concerned about inflation it demands a higher rate in order to offset inflation erosion. When the Fed lowers its rates fear of future inflation comes into play which may cause fixed rate mortgages to go up. Adjustable rate mortgages inherently deals with this problem as the rate is adjustable. A fixed rate cannot be adjusted later for inflation. Many times when the Fed lowers rates 30 year fixed mortgages go up as a result. This sounds a bit odd but is the nature of our economy. Understanding this can help you lock in a good interest rate.

Many times borrowers will put off refinancing or locking in a rate as they are watching the Fed lower rates hoping to get the lowest rate possible, only to see fixed rates go up. The reason is that the markets become concerned that inflation is not being fought off and could become a future problem. Remember that by the time financial news hits the public it usually is too late. That is why oftentimes people get into investments at their peak. They end up buying high and selling low. When considering locking your mortgage rate get ahead of the news. The coming reduction in rates the media is talking about probably means increased rates as the market reacts and speculates at the future implications of current financial news.

A word to the wise about adjustable rate mortgages, if you are considering an adjustable rate mortgage look at those that have a fixed term that outlives the time you expect to live in that home. If you are planning to sell your home in the next three years lock in a 5/1 or greater, this way if things don't go as planned you have a little more time on your side. Some adjustable rate mortgages have a fixed rate conversion option so that you can fix your rate without having to refinance for a small fee. However, it may still make sense to refinance as opposed to converting because you may get better pricing on the refinance. Do comparisons of interest rates between the two options, then calculate your savings in monthly mortgage payment versus the costs of one or the other.

Understanding how the financial markets affect interest rates will be helpful to you in targeting your interest rate. While most look to the 10 year treasury as the leading indicator to track the 30 year fixed mortgage rates you would be better served watching mortgage backed securities. The 10 year treasury is affected by demand for it which may not necessarily mean that there is demand for mortgage backed securities. Your mortgage note will become a mortgage backed security (MBS) and it is demand for MBS that has a direct impact on fixed interest rates. Other factors do affect MBS which in turn affect the rates offered by mortgage lenders. Case and point: investors turned to treasury bonds during our current economic crisis which is driving yield down due to high demand. However, demand is not as great for MBS currently due to the uncertainty of the mortgage market.

Your mortgage representative should be watching MBS as the leading indicator of mortgage rates. If they do not understand how to track MBS consider working with a mortgage professional that does.

CHAPTER 8

MORTGAGE PLANNING BASICS

Homeownership has many benefits. Most of us can attest to the improved quality of life we experience from owning our own home. The enjoyment and pride we take in our homes aside, there are some significant financial advantages to homeownership. As homeowners you will reduce your tax burden as you are able to deduct mortgage interest, property taxes and mortgage insurance. Additionally, you are able to participate in the appreciation of the real estate market. Over time real estate has proven to be an excellent investment. Three powerful dynamics are combining to build your wealth.

Understanding that homeownership and your mortgage should be an integral part of your overall financial planning will help you to maximize the financial benefits of homeownership and complement financial planning strategies for retirement, college planning and all aspects of your financial plan. Working with a Certified Mortgage Planning Specialist is a good way to better ensure that your mortgage is being approached with an understanding of your overall financial needs.

Oftentimes, borrowers shop for mortgages with only two things in mind, getting the approval and the lowest rate. If you talk to people who have been through the mortgage application process you will soon find out that there are a lot of horror stories out there. A lender who gives you a quick prequalification and shoots off the lowest rate without delving carefully into your qualifications will lead you down a path of surprises. You may find that your prequalification was worthless and may have spent money on inspections only to find out you don't qualify. Many times the rate, program and terms change as your lender gets to know you better. This can leave you pressed to take a higher rate or in a program that you might not have opted for if you weren't so far down the path. Understanding that program and rate is not a one size fits all proposition you will know that when someone quotes you or offers you a super rate that perhaps these are not deliverable or applicable to your specific situation. A wise approach in determining who you will hire to provide your mortgage financing is to work with a mortgage professional that has come to you by referral. Picking a lender randomly from an ad may not be the most prudent way to ensure a positive mortgage experience.

Could you imagine calling your doctor because you have pain in your right arm and he says, "no need to come in, I don't need to do any tests or examinations just take two aspirins and call me in the morning." If this doctor took this approach to diagnosing and treating everyone that called in he would be accused of being irresponsible and the patient foolish for not seeking competent care.

So it is when folks are shopping for a mortgage. They want the lowest rate and advise, experience and reputation are not a concern. When investing your savings getting the highest return on your dollars is important, however so are safety, term and liquidity. Similar concerns should be considered when shopping for a mortgage. While rate is important, so are terms, costs and integrating this large liability into the overall scheme of your short and long term financial goals. If your overall financial plan is not factored into your mortgage planning you may ultimately find yourself in credit card debt or repeatedly refinancing to pay for all the things that you haven't prepared for. While paying off your mortgage in 30 years is a valid concern so are all the things that fall in between. Establishing an emergency fund, taking steps to position you not to be credit dependent, establishing a college saving plan for your children and properly funding a retirement plan take precedent over paying off the 30 year mortgage, otherwise you will pay down the mortgage only to recast it later. This is what happens to so many homeowners. As a result home equity is consumed and depleted as they borrow thousands to pay for things in real time. Funding your future will position you to pay pennies on the dollar as opposed to dollars on the pennies. It is important to protect this wealth building asset known as your home. Careful planning to ensure its maximum benefit to you should be accounted for. Let's take a look at how your home can make you rich.

AMORTIZATION

The first dynamic is *amortization* which occurs as you are making your mortgage payments and reducing your mortgage balance, this translates to equity. Equity is your portion of real ownership in the home. Your objective over time is to reduce the liability while increasing equity. This is something you will never have if your housing payment is rent. Rent will only build equity for your landlord. Paying down your mortgage in effect is a forced savings plan. Americans have become bad savers and for many this is the only way to ensure and afford a savings plan.

With higher costs of living depending on Social Security just won't cut it. Additionally, pensions are a thing of the past. The equity that you build by homeownership can make a very positive impact on your present and future lifestyle. For many seniors today accessing that equity is allowing them to better enjoy the longer lives that they are blessed to live.

LEVERAGE

The second is *leverage*. When you invest in real estate you use a small amount of money to control a larger asset. If you have ten thousand dollars to invest you might look to open a money market account, savings account or mutual fund. If you are able to get a 5% return on your investment you will have earned $500.00 at the end of one year. Not bad. Unfortunately, this is more than likely taxable so your actual after tax return will be less than the 5% you earned. If you had invested that same ten thousand as a down payment on the purchase of a $200,000 home and your home appreciated 5% in its first year the value of your home would be $210,000. Your down payment of $10,000 controls the appreciation on the $200,000 asset. This is called leverage. In effect you have yielded a 100% return on your initial $10,000 investment and you now have $22,123.69 in equity assuming your mortgage is at 6.5%. This equity is comprised of your original investment, appreciation and the amortized principal. The power of the appreciation is magnified only because of the leverage component of real estate. Few people are able to pre-fund an investment with hundreds of thousands of dollars, but in effect this is what happens when you buy real estate. The day you purchase your home an asset potentially equal to twenty times your initial investment is added to your personal financial balance sheet. It would take a lifetime to save hundreds of thousands of dollars for most people. With homeownership you can control that asset early and enjoy its appreciation over the time.

COMPOUNDING

The third is the phenomenon known as *compounding*. Future

appreciation is now on a $210,000 value so your appreciation grows along with the base price of your home. Of course, as with any tangible asset appreciation can vary and there may be times of no growth or even depreciation. However, over time you will see why a home in 1957 that would have costs your parents $2,300, which was the average price of a home at that time, might be worth $250,000 today. This would represent growth of over 9% per year or a greater than 16% return on your original investment of only 5% of the asset value. In effect compounding has resulted in this asset increasing a hundred fold.

Investments that yield a return are typically taxable now or at a later time. Your home can grow and compound in value and when you sell it the difference in the price you paid and what you sell for minus costs of improvement and transfer costs is your profit. So long as you have lived in your home for at least 2 out the last 5 years, in most cases under current tax code you do not have to pay tax on your gain. This is an investment that is hard to match.

We spent some time discussing the importance of affordability in earlier chapters. This should be your foundational concern as you consider your finance options. Be honest in determining how much mortgage you can comfortably and successfully carry. If your mortgage payment will be three times your rent payment the likelihood is that you will not be able to carry that mortgage payment. Only consider a substantially higher payment if you can identify that while you had a lower rent payment you had money left over that enabled you to save or pay off debt.

Ensuring the proper financial planning by incorporating mortgage planning will protect this valuable investment which will build wealth for you while providing interim and long term quality of life benefits. This is an asset and investment that should be protected by careful planning. Additionally, when considering your affordability you should factor in the tax benefits in order to see what you truly can afford. This will give you an upward bump in housing payment affordability.

TAX IMPLICATIONS

Factor your tax savings as this will afford you more home without more personal income. Whenever we buy anything we buy with after tax dollars or take home pay. Consider this when you make any purchase. The worst illustration of this is when we apply this reality to our credit card debt. If we have 10k in credit card debt our monthly minimum payment will be about $300 per month. In order to have the cash to pay for this bill we would need to earn $450 or so to net $300. This could mean a full weeks pay for some. Now you send off the $300 only to see your balance reduced by $100. So in effect someone earning $22,000 annually may have worked a full week for $100 dollars or $2.50 per hour. And the $100 does nothing for your quality of life as it goes to pay for a pair of shoes you no longer even own.

When obtaining mortgage financing you pay with pre-tax dollars. This enables you to afford your mortgage payment more comfortably. This is because you are able to deduct the interest on your mortgage, property taxes and in most cases mortgage insurance. This means that if you have a proven record of paying $1500 per month in rent you should be able to pay an amount greater than that depending on what tax bracket you are in. Your mortgage payment reduces your taxable income which means you will either get a larger tax refund or more take home pay. Someone in a 25% bracket could reduce their tax bill and might be able to afford a mortgage payment of $1800-1900 as comfortably as their $1500 rent payment.

This is because they pay for rent with after tax dollars which is your net take home pay, whereas a mortgage is paid for with pre-tax dollars or your gross pay. In effect the government is allowing you to keep more of your income so that you can afford a better quality of life. Additional benefits are that homeownership is promoted which increases tax revenue to local governments.

While it's good to know that you may be able to afford more home than you thought the problem is that your mortgage payment is due on the 1st of every month and your tax refund may not be received for another 12 months. A strategy can be employed to increase your net take home pay to help with this. You can do this by forgoing the higher tax refund and keeping your money now. By increasing the exemptions on your W-4 you can create more disposable income when you need it. Your 1040 is simply a reconciliation form which determines if you underpaid or overpaid your taxes over the course of the year. Nothing prevents you from fine tuning your tax bill and keep your money when you need it most, as opposed to sending it off to the government earning you 0% interest until you reclaim it.

If you do not need your tax savings to afford your mortgage payment directing this savings into a savings program for an emergency, college or retirement planning is another way that your home can help you build wealth. It would be wise to seek the advice of your accountant to determine how many exemptions you can claim without over claiming which could present you with an additional bill at tax time.

EMERGENCY PLAN

Always have an emergency plan. The foundation of this plan should be a savings account with at least 3 months living expenses. Consider how you would handle loss of employment or other financial hardship. Deciding your course of action now can help you act more quickly and less emotionally if the time arises. Will you take employment outside of your profession? Can you rely on friends or relatives for help? Will you sell off assets or borrow against retirement savings? Do you have appropriate life insurance and disability insurance? How quickly will you list the home for sale if you get into trouble?

Set priorities now and consider what you will pay or not pay to prevent the loss of your home. Many times people will just go down with the ship. Make provision now to be better prepared to handle the unexpected. If at all possible keep a line of credit opened on your home to maintain liquidity and protect your equity. We will discuss this in the next chapter.

PROTECTING YOUR EQUITY

Be careful to use your equity wisely. Equity is the difference between what you owe on your home and the value of it. Many people solve their debt problems by consolidating credit card, consumer debt, vacations and other things into their mortgage. The liabilities on your consumer debt are the result of purchasing depreciating assets and it is not good to consume your equity on depreciating assets.

Most people consolidate consumer debt into their mortgage with no plan to stay out of debt. The only time it makes sense to roll your debt into your mortgage is when you have a plan to stash your savings into a savings or investment account. By doing this you will position yourself not to rely on credit cards when you are hit with life's little or not so little surprises. The only way to get ahead is to pay for things with pennies on the dollars as opposed to paying dollars on the pennies. Consider the person who pays cash for their life needs without relying on credit. That $500 dishwasher costs exactly that, whereas the credit card user will pay many more times that for the same product. Funding your future now enables you to buy for pennies on the dollar as the $500 dishwasher may have only meant saving $400 or less because of the compounded interest you have been earning on your savings. What would you rather do, pay $400 for that $500 dishwasher or $2000 after you account for the interest charges on a financed purchase? The answer is obvious yet many will charge items to get a 10% discount and then pay 30% interest per year on that item until it is finally paid off. Most consumers are paying a premium for all of their goods and services as they are financing them. The only time to consider financing something is if there is a potential financial gain and the cost to borrow becomes your cost of doing business. Finance charges end up being many times more than the original cost of the item financed.

A mortgage plan that incorporates debt consolidation is not complete without a component that redirects dollars into a systematic and disciplined savings plan. Be very careful to implement safeguards against a vicious credit cycle. Many people refinance and then run up their cards again because they were not careful to use the new cash flow to buy cash and save for future emergencies. If there isn't enough cash to buy something now... wait. Be careful not to persuade yourself to buy now on credit and you'll pay it off when you get the next bill, it rarely works out. Oftentimes you will find that in waiting you may discover you may not need or even want the item any longer.

Only work with a mortgage professional who understands that a quick fix band aid approach to debt consolidation is not good for your long term financial needs.

CHAPTER 9

ADVANCED MORTGAGE PLANNING

Owning a home is smart in and of itself, however by employing advanced mortgage planning strategies you can maximize the financial benefits of homeownership. In this final chapter we discuss important strategies you can employ to get the highest tax benefits, leverage your equity and protect it.

ACQUISITION INDEBTEDNESS

Most people assume that all mortgage interest is tax deductible without qualification. This is only true of the interest that you pay on the original mortgage you took when you bought the home plus an additional $100,000 home equity deduction. Cash out from your equity is only tax deductible on the first one hundred thousand of equity you pull out. An example might be someone who puts $250,000 down payment on a $400,000 home financing $150,000. A tax deduction of interest paid on the first mortgage of $150,000 is available to this tax payer.

This borrower later refinances their home and pulls out an additional $150,000 for a total mortgage of $300,000, current tax law would allow for a deduction on the interest paid on $250,000 of the $300,000 mortgage. When buying a home consider the tax implications of how much or how little you should borrow. Also, a very important consideration if you are buying a second home with proceeds of a refinance on your primary home as you will be limited to a deduction on the interest on $100k. Obtaining the financing directly on the second home could position you for maximum tax benefits.

When considering how much to borrow you may find that it might be better to take a larger mortgage to establish acquisition indebtedness. Subsequently save your cash in an investment with cash flow to help defray the cost of a larger mortgage if necessary. Perhaps tax-free municipal bonds that will pay you tax free income which you can use to pay your mortgage, while maintaining the tax favored status of your mortgage.

Acquisition indebtedness is a tax planning strategy that you should be mindful of as you approach homeownership. Consider how this would affect someone who retires and buys their retirement home for cash. At some point they will look to pull money out of their retirement accounts where they will have a tax liability. Perhaps a better way would be to buy tax-free municipal bonds and get a mortgage establishing acquisition indebtedness.

The tax-free income would pay for the mortgage payment and the tax deduction from the mortgage would offset the tax liability resulting from withdrawals to your retirement plan.

"SIGNING YOUR LIFE AWAY"

When you buy a home you are presented with a stack of forms requiring your signature. Signing all of these forms is an intimidating and daunting experience. The most important of these forms are the settlement statement or the HUD-1, the Mortgage Note, and the Mortgage. The HUD-1 itemizes all of the costs incurred as a result of obtaining the mortgage and buying the home and reconciles all of the numbers for both the buyer and the seller. The mortgage note is your promise to pay back the money you are borrowing and the terms of that loan. However, your personal guarantee is not sufficient so you will have to mortgage your home by signing a mortgage document which collateralizes your loan.

The mortgage is the lien that gets recorded against the deed to your home. While you will own the home as it is deeded to you, when you mortgage your home you agree to allow a lien against the home.

This is where it gets interesting. The mortgage note that you sign is for the amount of loan you are promising to pay back. In most cases the loan is a percentage of the value of the home. As you amortize the loan your balance reduces and your equity position increases. The note is attached to a declining number. At the same time you collateralize this note, not with an amount equal to the note but equal to the full value of your home which is an appreciating asset, so in turn this is an increasing number. Therefore, as your balance goes down and your home appreciates the note and the mortgage move further apart reducing the banks risk in the loan. This transfers greater risk to the homeowner with a mortgage.

An example might be taking out a $200,000 loan on a $250,000 home. The banks risk is equal to the loan amount and your risk is limited to the equity you have or $50,000. However, the loan is secured by a mortgage on your $250,000 home and as you amortize and your home appreciates the banks risk is reduced and yours increases. A few years from now your home could be worth $300,000 and you might owe $175.000, now your risk position is $125,000. In the event of a default the bank will not foreclose to recover their loan and give you the difference. They will seize your home and are entitled to not only the money they loaned, but all of your equity too. Understanding this will help you consider how to build the equity in your home. In light of this making an extra principal payment on your mortgage may not be in your best interest. Blowing the money certainly is not the alternative, but directing those dollars into a liquid and guaranteed account may be a better strategy.

HOME EQUITY LINE OF CREDIT

It is advisable that all homeowners have, whenever possible an equity line of credit on their home. This is a revolving line of credit against your home with convenience checks that enable you to access your equity. The purpose of this is not to finance depreciating assets, but to create an immediate emergency fund and secondly protect their equity by creating liquidity. In the unfortunate event of financial hardship you would be able to access your equity and prevent foreclosure or better equip yourself financially to deal with your crisis. This could potentially buy you the time you would need to recover or sell your home at a fair price as opposed to losing your home or selling it hastily out of fear of losing it.

Many foreclosures could be avoided if the borrower could access a few months of mortgage payments. The borrower might have tens of thousands of dollars locked up in equity and not be able to come up with a few thousand to avoid foreclosure.

Having the line of credit available can help to protect your equity. Additionally, having a line of credit opened during a time of declining real estate provides liquidity to your equity protecting it from vanishing due to reduced home prices. You should only use the line of credit for emergencies or short term needs when you know that you can replenish the line. Using these dollars to leverage other investment opportunities may be another alternative, but great care and competent counsel should be employed.

While your home will appreciate in time increasing your equity position the equity in your home has a 0% rate of return. Your home will appreciate at the same rate whether you owe on it or not. As a matter of fact the greater the liability against it the more you are *leveraging* that investment freeing up dollars that can be directed at other opportunities. This could enable you to lump sum fund college or retirement planning or at least get a good jump on these important financial needs.

Consider that while you have a mortgage on your home there is risk attached to that asset. A safer way to pay your mortgage might be to not be in a hurry to sink additional cash into it as this increases your risk, while reducing the banks risk. The idea is not to spend any additional disposable income irresponsibly, but to use it where it counts most. It would be better to pay off higher rate loans and credit cards with your disposable income than to prepay your low rate tax favored mortgage. Why pay a liability with a net after tax rate of 4-5% when you can pay down an 18% credit card.

Also, using your disposable dollars to buy cash would be money well spent as opposed to prepaying your mortgage and not having the money to buy the dishwasher cash and relying on credit. Every time you prepay your mortgage you are building your equity position but are locking up those dollars at a 0% rate of return that is now subjected to risk as there is a lien on those dollars by the mortgage bank.

EQUITY OUTSIDE OF YOUR HOME

A better strategy is to set aside those dollars and build equity outside of the mortgage lien in an investment account. A mortgage at 6.5% has a net effective after tax rate of about 4.5% and so long as you can get better than that or close to it you are better off. There are strategies that you can employ where even if you are yielding less on your investments than your cost to borrow on your mortgage, you would be better off. It's important to work with mortgage and financial planners who understand the power of this concept. You can always use those dollars to pay down or pay off your mortgage later.

Paying a lower interest rate than you earn on your investment dollars is known as arbitrage and it's what banks do everyday. Borrow at a low cost and lend at a higher rate. If you employ this strategy and invest wisely your mortgage will be paid on schedule and you will amass a fortune on your investment dollars.

By keeping your equity outside of your home you will have greater diversification opportunities, greater liquidity and cash that is free from a lien. This is a safer way to manage your equity. Very few of us would consider depositing or growing assets that weren't liquid and that had a lien attached to it. Additionally, it is always prudent to consider diversification as it is never a good idea to have all of your eggs in one basket. Many homeowners consider their homes to be their nest egg. It's important to protect it by using basic investment practices.

Consider that most homeowners in a pinch will resort to pulling out equity. They may find themselves in a compromised financial situation and may be out of work or have some credit issues that may preclude them from financing. Real estate prices may be down or lending criteria tightened as it is now and they can't access their own money. It is very sad to see someone with equity trapped in their home that forces them into making adverse financial and lifestyle decisions they would not have made if they could access their equity.

The following illustration shows how you would be able to pay off your mortgage sooner by building your equity outside of your home. Over time you will amass a greater net worth than you would have using a traditional prepay method.

Creditor	Payment	Balance	To Be Paid Off
First Mortgage	1230	185000	185000
Second Mortgage	196	18000	18000
Credit Card	75	2500	2500
Credit Card	70	2000	2000
Student loan	0	0	0
Auto	375	12000	12000
Auto	275	5000	5000
Installment	0	0	0
Credit Card	300	10000	10000
Credit Card	60	1000	1000

$250,000 @ 6.5% 30 yr Fixed	$	1,580.17
Payments before	$	2,581.
New Payment	$	1,580.
Monthly Savings	$	1,001
ANNUAL SAVINGS	$	12,018

In this example the borrower refinanced by taking a $250,000 mortgage and consolidated debt to create cash flow. This cash flow is not left unattended where it will dissipate into a black hole, but redirected to create a buffer of disposable income so that the borrower doesn't go back to spending on credit. The balance of the cash flow is directed into an equity savings account to accumulate equity outside of the mortgage.

The borrower is maximizing tax benefits and has created cash flow of $1,001 per month. We are directing $700.00 into a conservative savings account and leaving the borrowers with $300.00 improved cash flow for spending money. Now when they go out for dinner or need a new hockey stick for their boy it doesn't go on a credit card. The $700.00 accumulates in a liquid account so if there is ever any financial trouble the borrower is able to access their equity. This equity is not under the lien of the mortgage bank and not subject to seizure if you fall behind on your mortgage.

ACCELERATING MORTGAGE PAYOFF

Assuming a 5% rate of return on your investment dollars in less than 15 years there is enough equity in your side account to pay off your mortgage well ahead of schedule. This is a great way to pay off your mortgage early without the risk of paying extra into your mortgage and lose access to those dollars. If you chose not to pay off your mortgage you could continue the plan. At the end of the term, you would have your home paid off and an additional $582,000 in savings. At that time you could generate $2425 per month in income from your savings account without having to use the equity in your home or your investment account.

Many homeowners find that after they have spent years paying their home off they need to use a reverse mortgage to supplement their retirement income. A reverse mortgage is the opposite of a traditional mortgage available to the senior community where equity can be accessed but a mortgage payment is not required. By building equity outside of your home and leveraging equity to yield a rate of return you would have a sizable nest egg outside of the nest from where you can draw your supplemental retirement income.

Another strategy that could work well for folks who do not have a lot of disposable income for retirement planning or who do not have matching contributions or a pension plan at work is investing in real estate. You can control a large asset with a small amount of money.

RETIRE ON REAL ESTATE

Consider buying an investment property annually or every other year. Do this 3-5 times and you can build a nice real estate portfolio that can fund your retirement. The properties can pay for themselves and in time will have an asset that you leveraged and is worth many times what you paid for it. Say you buy a home a year at an average price of $250k. You may be required to invest 10% or so which amounts to 25k in this example. Do this every year for 4 years and you are controlling a real estate portfolio of over a million dollars. Using the power of leverage you are compounding a rate of return on a million dollars while only having invested $100,000. While you are managing these homes you may create a positive cash-flow that will improve your quality of life and help to fund a Simple IRA or other retirement account.

Additionally, while real estate appreciates you will have the tax incentive known as depreciation where you can claim a loss in value of the home even though the home may be appreciating.

If you held on to this portfolio until retirement you might be paid up on your mortgages or close to it. The portfolio could be worth $1.8MM generating you a cash flow from the rents which you can live on. You may choose to sell and do what you want with your millions. Investing 100k can yield you millions by using the principals of amortization, leveraging and compounding.

Real Estate continues to be a good investment. There are many opportunities that are becoming available in increasing numbers in this post mortgage meltdown market. Whenever we look at a booming real estate or stock market we kick ourselves and wish we had gotten in on the ground level. Well the good news is that we are at or approaching ground level and there are many buying opportunities available. Timing markets is a dangerous thing, but certainly in light of how real estate has historically performed, current home values and the fact that you have to live somewhere anyway it may be a good idea to consider the many opportunities available to you today.

Be careful about buying on speculation in a quick flip type of deal in this market as inventory is slow to move, but buy and hold is certainly a smart approach. Consider other markets outside of your own as there are bargains out there that make it possible to buy and rent with a positive cash flow. Don't ever get into a negative cash flow situation.

Owning a home is something everyone hopes for. It fills us with a sense of pride and accomplishment. It gives us satisfaction to know that we have created a place where we can feel safe and enjoy our families and friends. Memories that will stay with us the rest of our lives are the result of fun and oftentimes challenging home improvement projects that bring our families closer together. We will bring our children into it, raise them and enjoy them in it. We will marry them off in it and enjoy our grandchildren in it. It's a good thing. Enjoy it and maximize all of its benefits: lifestyle and financial.

APPENDIX

Glossary

Adjustable Rate Mortgage (ARM): A mortgage with a rate that is or may become variable.

ALT-A: Mortgages that were classified alternative to "A" paper, but not sub-prime. This market developed to meet the needs of borrowers who didn't meet the conforming or FHA underwriting requirements, but were not sub-prime borrowers.

COFI: Cost of Funds Index is an average of the 11th district financial institutions interest expenses sometimes used as an index to determine the renewal rate of an adjustable rate mortgage.

COMMITMENT: A contractual date is set at time of contract where the buyer must obtain a lender commitment. This supercedes any pre-approval as the lender has reviewed all pertinent borrower data and has issued it's "commitment" to lend.

CONVENTIONAL LOAN: A loan that meets FNMA/FREDDIE MAC underwriting requirements and loan limits.

COLLATERALIZED DEBT OBLIGATION (CDO): A bond or debt obligation that is issued with underlying guarantees over and above personal or institutional as it is collateralized by a tangible asset.

CONSUMER PRICE INDEX (CPI): A measurement of the average cost of goods and services that is a leading indicator of economic health and inflationary direction

COSI: Cost of Savings index is an average of savings interest rates and is sometimes used as an index to determine adjustable rate mortgage renewal rates

ESCROW: 1.The period of time between the execution of a contract of sale and transfer of title. 2. Funds held by bank in your name to pay for future tax and insurance bills.

EQUITY: Ownership. This is the difference between what you owe and the value of your home or asset which is your true ownership.

DEBT TO INCOME RATIO (DTI): The percentage of monthly housing payment and consumer debt payments as it compares to your total income.

DESKTOP UNDERWRITING: Fannie Mae's automated underwriting model

DISCOUNT POINTS: This is a prepayment of interest in exchange for a lower interest rate.

FANNIE MAE: Federal National Mortgage Association which is a purchaser of mortgages and securitizes them to be sold on the open market

FED (FOMC): This is the Federal Open Market Committee, led by Ben Bernanke that sets monetary policy by directing the Fed Funds Interest Rate in an effort to maintain a healthy economy.

FED FUNDS RATE: An overnight loan rate for inter financial institution lending that is set by the FOMC

FHA: The Federal Housing Administration, a government agency which insures mortgages

FREDDIE MAC: Federal Home Loan Mortgage Corporation is a purchaser of mortgages and securitizes them to be sold on the open market

GINNIE MAE: Government National Mortgage Association guarantees MBS of federally insured loans

INTEREST ONLY: A mortgage only the interest is required to be paid. No principal is being collected so the principal balance remains the same.

JUMBO LOAN: A loan with a loan amount that exceeds FNMA limits.

LIBOR: London Inter-Bank Offered Rate which we is our Fed Funds Rate counterpart and is used as an index in determining adjustable rate mortgage renewal rates

LOAN TO VALUE (LTV): The percentage of loan amount as compared to the lesser of the appraised value or purchase price.

LOAN PROPECTOR (LP): Freddie Mac's automated underwriting model

MARGIN: An internal fixed rate within an adjustable mortgage that when added to the index sets the interest rate

MORTGAGE BACKED SECURITIES (MBS): A security that is collateralized whose cash flow is backed by payments on mortgages

MTA: an index that is an average of the monthly treasuries for the last 12 months.

NEGATIVE AMORTIZATION: A loan where the minimum payment is less than the interest portion of the mortgage payment resulting in a portion of the interest becoming deferred and added to the principal balance of your mortgage.

PRIME RATE: A standardized lending rate that some loans are set to, particularly Home Equity Lines of Credit

PRIVATE MORTGAGE INSURANCE: Insurance against the risk of potential default of the mortgage loan with the bank as the beneficiary. This coverage offsets a portion of the principal balance which reduces the risk to the bank

RATE LOCK: The interest rate that is locked or fixed for the life of the mortgage or for a period certain time frame on adjustable rate mortgages

REFINANCE: The recasting of your mortgage with a new set of terms for the purposes of modifying the terms of your loan known as a rate and term refinance or cashing equity out known as a cash-out refinance

SUB-PRIME: A class of mortgage for borrowers who are not able to meet conforming, FHA or ALT-A guidelines

TREASURY INDEX: An average of US Treasury securities that are adjusted to a constant 1 year maturity which is sometimes used as an index to determine the renewal rate of an adjustable rate mortgage

RESOURCES

Certified Mortgage Planning Institute
www.cmpsinstitute.org

Credit Bureaus
www.experian.com

www.transunion.com

www.equifax.com

Government Agencies
www.hud.gov

www.fanniemae.com

www.freddiemac.com

Mortgage Plus Home Loans
888-734-PLUS

www.mpfgonline.com

MORTGAGE FACTOR CHART

Factor per thousand borrowed

Rate	Interest Only	15 Year	20 Year	30 Year	40 Year
5.000	0.41667	7.90794	6.59956	5.36822	4.82197
5.125	0.42708	7.97320	6.66881	5.44487	4.90505
5.250	0.43750	8.03878	6.73844	5.52204	4.98870
5.375	0.44792	8.10465	6.80847	5.59971	5.07293
5.500	0.45833	8.17083	6.87887	5.67789	5.15770
5.625	0.46875	8.23732	6.94966	5.75656	5.24302
5.750	0.47917	8.30410	7.02084	5.83573	5.32888
5.875	0.48958	8.37118	7.09238	5.91538	5.41525
6.000	0.50000	8.43857	7.16431	5.99551	5.50214
6.125	0.51042	8.50625	7.23661	6.07611	5.58952
6.250	0.52083	8.57423	7.30928	6.15717	5.67740
6.375	0.53125	8.64250	7.38232	6.23870	5.76575
6.500	0.54167	8.71107	7.45573	6.32068	5.85457
6.625	0.55208	8.77994	7.52950	6.40311	5.94385
6.750	0.56250	8.84909	7.60364	6.48598	6.03357
6.875	0.57292	8.91854	7.67814	6.56929	6.12373
7.000	0.58333	8.98828	7.75299	6.65302	6.21431
7.125	0.59375	9.05831	7.82820	6.73719	6.30531
7.250	0.60417	9.12863	7.90376	6.82176	6.39672
7.375	0.61458	9.19923	7.97967	6.90675	6.48852
7.625	0.63542	9.34130	8.13254	7.07794	6.67327
7.750	0.64583	9.41276	8.20949	7.16412	6.76620

For example if you are borrowing $200, 000 at 6.250% for 30 years find the corresponding factor and multiply by 200. This will give you the monthly mortgage payment to which you will add taxes and homeowners insurance. Also, factor in mortgage insurance if it applies. If you are obtaining an FHA loan the mortgage insurance factor is .55. Multiply the loan amount by .55 and divide by 12. Conforming loans will have varying rates depending on the percentage of down payment.

DOCUMENT CHECKLIST

INCOME

- ❏ Signed tax returns – last 2 years all schedules
- ❏ Copy of last 2 years W-2's
- ❏ Copy of pay stubs
- ❏ Document any pay stub loans
- ❏ Resume of work history for 2 years
- ❏ Pension award letter
- ❏ Court order for alimony/child support
- ❏ Child's birth certificate if receiving child support
- ❏ Evidence of last 12 months history for child support/ alimony

CREDIT

- ❏ Credit reports

- ❑ Credit explanation letter
- ❑ Bankruptcy paperwork w/ discharge
- ❑ Evidence collection and charged off accounts paid
- ❑ Warrant of satisfaction for any paid judgments
- ❑ Alternative account payment history letter
- ❑ Rental payment history and landlord information

ASSETS

- ❑ Bank statements
- ❑ Explain and source any large deposits
- ❑ Brokerage statements
- ❑ Retirement account statements
- ❑ Copy of check for down payment

MISC.

- ❑ Social Security Card
- ❑ Driver's license
- ❑ Green card
- ❑ Work Visa
- ❑ CPA letter/ business license if self employed

DEBT TO INCOME WORKSHEET

Proposed Housing Debt	
Principal & Interest	
Secondary Financing	
Homeowner's Insurance	
Flood Insurance	
Property Taxes	
Association Dues	
TOTAL	

Income	
Wages	
Business Income 2year average	
Overtime 2 year average	
Commission 2 year average	
Pension – retirement – social security	
Child Support/ Alimony > 3 years remaining	
Rental @ .75	
TOTAL	

Consumer Debt	
Credit Card Minimum Payments	
Student Loans w/ less than 12 mos. Deferral	
Auto Payment w/ more than 10 pays left	
Installment Loan Payments w/ more than 10 pays left	
Auto Lease Payments	
Child Support/Alimony	
TOTAL	

Housing Debt _____/ _____ Income = _____ Front Ratio

Consumer Debt _____ + _____Housing Debt =_____Total

Total _____ / _____ Income = _____Back Ratio

FRONT _____ BACK _____

DEBT RATIO REDUCTION WORKSHEET

INSTALLMENT DEBT	Monthly Payment x 10	Difference
Car loan 5,000.00	$375 x 10 = $3,750.00	$1,250.00

Difference = amount required to eliminate debt from ratio calculation

Minimum Payment (A)	Revolving Credit (B)	Divide (A) by (B)
Credit card $78.00	Balance $2,500	.0312

Pay off the accounts that produce the highest payment rate factor first.

Louis Soto, CMPS®

Mortgage Plus Financial Group

67 Walnut Avenue

Clark, NJ 07066

848-467-3100

louis@mpfgonline.com

www.ingramcontent.com/pod-product-compliance
Lightning Source LLC
Chambersburg PA
CBHW031245280526
45784CB00004B/1728